THE EXIT INTERVIEW FOR STRESS

A Field Guide for HR Pros
(and Everyone Else Who Holds Too Much)

JASON MICHAELS,
MBA, SPHR, SHRM-CP

Published by **Jason Michaels Publishing**
Rocky Mount, Virginia, USA

ISBN: 9798994187609

First Edition, 2025

For more resources, updates, and author information, visit:
www.thejasonmichaels.com

Printed in the United States of America

Disclaimer

This book is based on the author's personal and professional experience in the field of Human Resources. It is intended for informational and reflective purposes only and does not constitute legal, medical, psychological, or financial advice.

While every effort has been made to present practical tools and insights, the author makes no guarantees of specific outcomes. Readers are encouraged to use their own judgment and seek appropriate professional support when needed.

Any resemblance to actual individuals, situations, or organizations is purely coincidental unless explicitly stated.

Dedication

To my family — your love has carried me through every chapter of this HR journey.

To my wife, Alicia — your steady encouragement, unwavering belief, and grace have made all of this possible. I wouldn't be here without you.

To my son Jonathan — you are my daily reminder that the future is worth investing in.

To my son Thomas — your impact on my thinking and growth is undeniable. You've shaped more of these pages than you may ever know.

And to Megan Pittman — thank you for seeing the value in my perspective, for supporting my voice, and for giving me the confidence to turn experience into something that might help others.

This book exists because you all poured into me. I hope it now pours into someone else.

Contents

Foreword

I didn't write this book because I mastered stress. I wrote it because I nearly let it take me out.

Twelve years in HR taught me that people don't just bring their resumes to work—they bring their fear, grief, trauma, burnout, and every personal emergency in between. And more often than not, they bring it to HR.

We're expected to be calm, neutral, strong. We're told to "be there" but never "bring it home." But what happens when you've been "there" for everyone and there's nothing left for you?

That question haunted me for years. I didn't have a breakdown or a dramatic exit. I just got really tired. I lost my joy. I felt numb. And I started to wonder if maybe HR just wasn't for me anymore.

But what I realized was this: HR didn't break me — how I was doing HR did. I was carrying too much. I was confusing compassion with self-sacrifice. I was absorbing everything and pretending it wasn't affecting me.

This book is the one I wish I had earlier in my career. It's not about quitting the field. It's about quitting the unhealthy patterns that are silently burning us out.

It's about giving yourself permission to breathe, to pause, to say "that's not mine to carry." It's about learning how to stay in this work without losing yourself.

If you're feeling the weight, this book is your signal: it's time to put it down.

You deserve peace — not just outside of work, but inside it, too.

Let's begin.

— *Jason Michaels, MBA, SPHR, SHRM-CP*

Chapter 1
The Emotional Sponge Effect

Twelve years in HR and I can tell you this: we absorb more than we ever admit. The stress, the complaints, the politics, the awkward conversations, the terminations, the crying-in-the-breakroom moments—they all end up in us. It's like we're human shock absorbers for everyone else's pain. And if you don't stop and ask yourself what you're holding, you'll start to believe it's all yours.

I call it the Emotional Sponge Effect. You walk into work with good intentions and a clear head, and within an hour, you've soaked up three grievances, a harassment allegation, and someone's panic attack. HR professionals are trained to listen, support, stay calm—but where does all that energy go? Straight into our nervous systems.

And here's the kicker: we've normalized it. We wear our burnout like a badge. We hustle for everyone else's comfort while putting our own wellness on the back burner. We tell ourselves it's part of the job. But here's what I want to challenge in this chapter: it's not.

Yes, empathy is a gift. Yes, we need to be emotionally intelligent. But no, we do not need to carry the emotional residue of every meeting, meltdown, and policy update. That's not sustainable, and it's not noble. It's self-erasure.

This chapter is about calling that out. Owning what we've been doing unconsciously. It's about realizing how deep the Emotional Sponge Effect runs and what it's costing us.

How It Starts

It usually doesn't hit all at once. It creeps in. One minute you're coaching a manager on conflict resolution, the next you're mediating a shouting match between team leads. And somewhere in there, you skipped lunch, sat through a 90-minute meeting that could have been an email, and checked your inbox 42 times.

You don't even realize you're holding tension in your shoulders or clenching your jaw until the day ends and your body feels like a locked vault.

This slow buildup is dangerous because it tricks us into thinking we're fine. We adapt. We get used to the emotional labor. But long-term? It eats at our health, our joy, and our sense of self.

The Invisible Job Inside the Job

What most people outside our profession don't get is that there are two HR jobs: the one on paper, and the one that lives in the emotional undercurrent. That second one? That's the real drain.

On paper: compliance, hiring, strategy, payroll, DEI. In reality: absorbing trauma, resolving emotional drama, absorbing toxicity so it doesn't poison the team.

We are the silent first responders of the workplace. But unlike medics or firefighters, no one expects us to debrief. There's no protocol for releasing what we take in. So we carry it. Until we break.

HR becomes the unofficial therapist, mediator, and fixer because no one else is trained—or willing—to hold the space for discomfort. And the moment we show even the slightest capacity to listen without judgment, people latch on. They bring us the pieces of themselves they can't show their boss, their team, or sometimes even their family.

I learned this fast. Maybe a month into my first role as an HR generalist, an employee came in and asked to talk. I was the only one available. Twenty minutes later, I found myself deep in a conversation I never expected: they told me they felt completely out of options and like they were heading down a dark road. I wasn't prepared. I was trying everything I could to gently steer the conversation toward something safe, something actionable. I knew about our resources—our incredible employee assistance program—but in that moment, I was just a human trying to keep someone from tipping over the edge.

Eventually, I managed to guide the conversation to the EAP, and they agreed to give it a try. That employee got the support they needed. They're still with the company today. Thriving. Not just professionally—personally too. But I carried that conversation for a long time. Not because it broke me, but because it opened my eyes. This is the part of the job nobody tells you about. It's not in the onboarding manual.

And that's why this work is so heavy: we don't just manage policies. We manage people's turning points. Their stress. Their survival.

Naming It Is the First Step

Let's name it now. You're not weak for feeling overwhelmed. You're not bad at your job for needing space. You are not failing for wanting to unplug. What's happening is that you've been absorbing everyone else's weight, and now you need to put it down.

In the chapters ahead, we're going to talk about how. We'll build the skills, boundaries, and mindsets to unplug from what isn't yours and re-center in what is.

But for now, I want you to do one thing:

Breathe.

Not a shallow, keyboard breath. A real one. In through your nose. Out through your mouth. Again. Because this is where it starts: with presence. With you. With reclaiming your nervous system.

You don't have to hold it all. You never did.

Welcome to the release.

Chapter 2
The Myth of the Unshakeable Professional

Let's be real — HR has a branding problem. We're expected to be calm under pressure, diplomatic in chaos, and emotionally bulletproof no matter what hits the fan. Somewhere along the line, we internalized the belief that showing emotion equals losing credibility.

But who decided that professionalism meant emotional suppression?

There's this unspoken myth in HR: if you're rattled, you're not ready. If you need help, you're weak. If you cry, you're crossing a line. So we armor up. We speak in measured tones. We master the poker face. We nod politely through absurdity and gaslight ourselves into thinking we're "fine."

But that myth? It's costing us.

It's creating guilt around being human. It's shaming us for needing boundaries. It's making us feel like we can't admit when something cuts too deep. And over time, that constant internal filtering wears you down.

Where the Myth Comes From

The myth of the unshakeable HR professional didn't come from nowhere. It was handed to us by outdated leadership models, toxic work cultures, and generations of emotional silence in the workplace.

We watched the people before us stay late, speak softly, and never complain. We took notes. We learned that strength meant self-denial. And now we repeat the pattern — until it breaks us.

But let's be honest: there is nothing professional about selfdestruction. There is nothing weak about needing rest, asking for support, or acknowledging that something affected you deeply.

What It Really Means to Be Strong in HR

Strength isn't stoicism. Strength is knowing your limits. It's staying grounded when things get messy. It's holding space for someone else's breakdown without abandoning yourself in the process.

True professionalism is presence. It's clarity. It's showing up as a full human being who has the skill to navigate hard conversations without pretending they don't hurt.

You can be empathetic and firm. You can be kind and direct. You can be compassionate and clear. And you can absolutely be a strong HR professional without being emotionally numb.

This chapter is your permission slip to feel. To shake. To not always have the perfect response. To be a professional — and a person.

The myth is just that. A myth. Let's stop living under it.

Chapter 3

Death by a Thousand Micro-Stressors

Burnout doesn't usually show up as a dramatic collapse. It creeps in, quietly and constantly — like water dripping on stone. Over time, it wears you down. And in HR, those drips come from everywhere.

Someone drops by your desk to vent. A manager needs help addressing "a situation." An employee asks about a policy you literally just explained last week. You finally sit down to tackle a strategic initiative and your inbox explodes. None of it seems like a big deal in isolation — but added together, these micro-stressors become a full-blown emotional overload.

We don't talk enough about this. The friction of a normal HR day. The low-grade, ever-present pressure that never fully lets up. And because it's not one massive crisis, we dismiss it.

"Oh, it's just part of the job." "It wasn't that bad." "I should be able to handle this."

But that "should" is a lie. You're human. A thousand little interruptions, irritations, and invisible demands take a toll — whether you acknowledge it or not.

The Energy Leak No One Sees

Micro-stress is sneaky because it's socially acceptable. You can't always say no. You don't want to seem unavailable or unhelpful. So you stay "on." All day. Every day.

Your brain doesn't get a break. You switch contexts constantly. One minute you're thinking about open enrollment, the next you're resolving a personality clash, and then it's time for layoffs. Again. That mental whiplash burns energy fast.

This constant shifting pulls from your reserves. And unless you're actively refueling, you start running on fumes — even though it looks like you're functioning fine from the outside.

The Trap of Constant Availability

One of the biggest micro-stress culprits in HR? The unspoken expectation that you're always available. Always ready. Always responsive.

You become the default help desk, crisis line, and walking policy manual. And if you don't set boundaries (more on that in Chapter 4) , you can spend entire days in reactive mode — never getting to the work that actually fulfills you.

Naming Your Patterns

Take a minute and look at your last week. Not the big fires, but the low-level stuff:

- How many times were you interrupted?

- How many mini-problems landed in your lap?

- How often did you mentally switch gears?

- How much time did you spend just recovering from the day?

It adds up. It matters.

And the first step is simply this: **recognize that these micro-stressors are real**. They deserve your attention. They explain your fatigue. And they are not your fault.

Reclaiming Your Bandwidth

You can't eliminate every stressor — but you can create space. You can build recovery time into your day. You can design your calendar like your energy matters. Because it does.

Simple strategies that make a big difference:

- **Schedule "no meeting" zones** — Protect sacred time for focus.

- **Batch similar tasks** — Stop the constant mental gear-switching.

- **Default to async** — Push back on unnecessary live calls.

- **Name the stressor** — Saying "this feels like a lot" can be enough to shift your mindset and reclaim agency.

HR doesn't have to be constant chaos. But if we don't interrupt the pattern, the pattern will interrupt us.

This chapter isn't about fixing everything. It's about validating what's real — and reminding you that your peace is worth prioritizing.

On to boundaries next.

Chapter 4

Boundaries That Actually Hold

In HR, boundaries aren't optional — they're survival.

The problem is, most of us weren't taught how to build them in a way that actually holds. We were taught to be helpful, responsive, and

supportive. We took pride in being "available" — until availability became expectation. Until every ping, tap, and "got a minute?" slowly chipped away at our peace.

This chapter is where we reclaim it.

The Line Between Empathy and Over-Functioning

Empathy is essential in HR. It's what makes us human. But when empathy morphs into over-functioning, we cross a dangerous line — from connection into depletion.

Over-functioning looks like:

- Taking on emotional labor that isn't yours

- Doing the work someone else was supposed to do

- Feeling guilty when you can't fix something

- Anticipating everyone's needs before they ask

These patterns are often praised. "You're so reliable." "We couldn't do this without you." But the truth? Over-functioning is unsustainable. It trains others to depend on your burnout. And it hides the fact that your own needs are going unmet.

The job isn't to carry everyone. It's to help them stand on their own.

Saying No Without Guilt

"No" doesn't make you cold. "No" doesn't make you difficult. "No" makes your "yes" sustainable.

Here's what we often forget: when you say yes to everything, you're saying no to something else — usually your own priorities, mental clarity, or even lunch.

It's not about rejecting people. It's about respecting your capacity.

Try these mindset shifts:

- "Protecting my energy makes me more effective, not less."

- "I can care without carrying."

- "My boundary is an invitation for others to grow."

Scripts for Real-Life Boundary Moments

Boundaries get tested when you're tired. That's why you need *go-to language* ready — so you're not caught off guard and guilted into overextending.

Here are a few simple, respectful scripts to keep in your back pocket:

The Calm Redirect: "I want to give this the attention it deserves — can we schedule a time instead of squeezing it in right now?"

The Capacity Check: "I'm currently at capacity and wouldn't be able to give this my full attention. Is it time-sensitive, or can we revisit?"

The Ownership Reminder: "I'm here to support you in finding a solution — but I can't take this on for you."

The Policy Reframe: "I know this might not be the answer you were hoping for, but I have to stay aligned with what's fair and consistent."

Boundaries are best enforced calmly and early. You don't need to over-explain. You don't need to apologize. You just need to be clear and kind

— and hold the line even when it's uncomfortable.

Boundary Fatigue Is Real

Saying no isn't always the hard part. Holding the no is.

You might feel guilty. You might worry what people will think. But the cost of a porous boundary is far higher than the discomfort of enforcing one.

And if someone pushes back, that doesn't mean you've done something wrong — it just means the boundary was necessary.

Letting Go of What's Not Yours

Every time you step in to absorb something that isn't yours, you rob someone else of the opportunity to learn, lead, or be responsible for their part.

You are not the fixer of all things. You are not the emotional landfill for unresolved workplace issues. You are a professional with limits, and honoring them is not selfish — it's a service to yourself and the people you support.

Your role is important. But your wellbeing is not negotiable.

Let the next chapter be your permission to release what was never yours to carry in the first place.

Chapter 5
You're Not the System

Let's say it plain: *You didn't break the system — so stop thinking it's your job to hold it together alone.*

HR professionals are often the face of policies they didn't write, structures they didn't design, and decisions they had no say in. And yet, when those things fall apart, who gets the side-eyes, the venting, the loaded "can we talk?" meetings?

We do.

And because we care — because we're wired for accountability — we internalize it. We take the blame. We over-own. We silently shoulder the dysfunction of systems that existed long before we walked in the door.

But here's the truth: **you're not the system**. You work *inside* it. You *navigate* it. You *influence* it — but you didn't build it, and you don't control it.

Letting Go of the Blame

One of the heaviest weights HR pros carry is invisible blame — for other people's poor leadership, broken communication loops, or long-ignored culture problems. When an employee tells you, "This place is toxic," they're often not talking about you — but you feel responsible anyway.

That's empathy at work. But it can morph into shame if you don't keep it in check.

You are not personally responsible for fixing everything that's wrong with the organization. That's not your burden. That's the system's work —

and it's a shared responsibility.

Letting go of blame doesn't mean giving up. It means getting honest about your role, your reach, and your limits.

When the Problem Is Cultural, Not Personal

One of the most freeing realizations you can have in HR is this: *Sometimes the system is sick — not you.*

If you find yourself constantly second-guessing your instincts, wondering if you're "too sensitive," or questioning your competence even though you're working yourself to the bone — step back.

Ask:

- Are the expectations on me realistic?

- Am I being supported, or just managed?

- Am I reacting to a broken culture, not a personal failing?

Many HR professionals burn out not because they're bad at their jobs, but because they're functioning in environments that reward self-abandonment. Where speaking up gets labeled as "difficult," and advocating for balance feels like rocking the boat.

You cannot heal a culture by bleeding yourself dry for it.

You can model something better. You can name what's unhealthy. You can influence upward. But if the system resists change, that's not your fault.

Stop Owning Outcomes You Can't Control

Here's a tough but necessary truth: *You can do everything "right" and still not get the outcome you hoped for.*

You can write a perfect policy. Facilitate a thoughtful conflict mediation. Support a struggling employee with care and consistency. And things can still fall apart.

You are responsible for the process — not the outcome.

Owning outcomes you can't control is a fast track to frustration and burnout. It creates a false sense of failure that chips away at your confidence. And it's not fair.

Instead, redefine success:

- Did I act with integrity?

- Did I communicate clearly?

- Did I offer tools, resources, or pathways forward?

- Did I maintain my own boundaries and well-being?

If the answer is yes, *you did your job*. Whether the other party chooses to change, engage, or evolve — that's theirs to carry.

Refusing to Be the Buffer

HR often becomes the buffer between employees and leadership, between dysfunction and accountability. We're asked to soften blows, explain away decisions, and "help people understand."

But being a buffer means absorbing impact that was never meant for you.

You don't have to put yourself in the crossfire to be effective.

Instead, shift from buffer to *translator*. Help others make sense of what's happening, yes — but don't absorb the damage. Name the system when it's at fault. Let consequences land where they belong.

What You Are Responsible For

You're not the system — but you *are* a powerful part of it.

You're responsible for:

- Speaking truth, even when it's inconvenient

- Modeling the boundaries you advocate for

- Holding space without becoming the container

- Redirecting blame to where it belongs

- Leading with empathy *and* clarity

Most of all, you're responsible for protecting your peace while doing the best work you can with what you've got.

You're not failing. You're functioning in a flawed machine.

So step back. Breathe. Zoom out.

The system needs change — but it doesn't need to cost you your sanity.

Let's keep going.

Chapter 6

Dismantling the Hero Complex

There's a part of HR that feels like a secret mission. You see things others don't. You step in quietly to prevent disaster. You know how to diffuse, de-escalate, redirect. And when it works, people rarely even notice.

You're the backstage fixer. The silent stabilizer. The one who makes sure everything holds together.

It's noble. It's honorable.

But it's also unsustainable.

And if you're not careful, it turns into something dangerous: the *hero complex*.

The Trap of Trying to Save Everyone

Here's how it usually starts: someone comes to you in distress. A manager is struggling. A team is imploding. Leadership is making another questionable decision. And without even thinking, you jump in.

"I'll handle it."

"Let me take this off your plate."

"I'll fix it before it gets worse."

You don't do it for recognition. You do it because you care. Because you're competent. Because no one else is stepping up.

But soon, your days start filling with problems that aren't yours. You begin measuring your value by how many fires you put out. You become reactive instead of strategic — because the emergencies never stop.

Saving everyone starts to look like your job. And your actual job— your *real* purpose — gets lost in the smoke.

You Are Not the Rescuer

Let's be clear: **you are not the hero**. You're the *guide*.

Rescuers remove discomfort. Guides walk with people through it.

Rescuers take on the problem. Guides help others find their own solution.

Rescuers make things easier in the short term — and accidentally create dependency. Guides ask hard questions, hold boundaries, and foster growth.

Your job isn't to protect people from every bad experience. It's to help them navigate those experiences with dignity and direction.

The hero complex says: "If I don't step in, everything will fall apart."

The healthy HR pro says: "If I step back, others might finally step up."

Why It Leads to Burnout

The more you carry, the more people expect you to carry. The hero complex rewards over-functioning with more dysfunction. It attracts chaos. It reinforces the idea that other people can offload their responsibility onto you.

And when you finally drop the weight? The system blames you for letting it fall.

Burnout isn't always from doing too much — sometimes it's from doing *too much of what isn't yours*.

You don't just get tired. You get resentful. Detached. Numb.

That's your signal. That's the moment to ask:

- Am I stepping in because it's necessary — or because I don't trust others to handle it?

- Am I helping — or enabling?

- Am I leading — or rescuing?

Letting People Sit with Discomfort

This is one of the hardest skills to learn in HR: **watching someone struggle without immediately intervening.**

Sometimes the most supportive thing you can do is nothing.

Let them process. Let them problem-solve. Let them feel what they need to feel.

Growth doesn't happen in comfort. And your role isn't to block discomfort — it's to create space where people can move *through* it with safety and accountability.

You can still be empathetic. You can still care deeply. But you can't keep throwing yourself in front of every emotional bullet and expect to survive the job.

Reframing Your Identity

You're not weak for stepping back. You're wise.

Stepping out of the hero role doesn't mean you stop helping. It means you help *differently* — with discernment, not desperation.

Your job isn't to save the company. Your job is to bring clarity, fairness, and humanity *into* the company.

That doesn't require a cape. It requires boundaries. It requires trust. And it requires the courage to lead in ways that don't drain you dry.

You're not here to be the hero.

You're here to change the story.

And that starts with letting go of the one where you had to do it all.

Chapter 7

The Power of Mental Clarity

Let's not sugarcoat it: HR can feel like mental gymnastics on a balance beam — blindfolded.

By noon, your brain's already juggled a termination, a birthday card, a grievance, a miscommunication between teams, and an executive who suddenly thinks you're in charge of employee morale. It's not just busy — it's *fragmented*.

And that fragmentation? It's a quiet threat. Not just to your focus, but to your well-being.

This chapter is about reclaiming the one resource you can't afford to lose: *mental clarity.*

Because when your mind is scattered, foggy, or constantly hijacked, you don't just lose time. You lose presence. You lose confidence. You lose connection to the part of you that knows what matters most.

So let's build it back — ten minutes at a time.

Quick Daily Tools to Reset

You don't need an hour-long mindfulness retreat. You need something you can do today — between back-to-back meetings or right before you spiral.

Here are three tools that can help reset your mind in five to ten minutes:

1. Breathwork (Yes, It Works)

Stress shortens the breath. Short breath signals danger. Your nervous system tightens. And your thinking narrows — which is the opposite of clarity.

Try this reset:

- Inhale through your nose for 4 seconds

- Hold for 4 seconds

- Exhale slowly through your mouth for 6–8 seconds

- Repeat 3–5 cycles

This isn't "woo." It's nervous system regulation. You're telling your body, "We're safe. We're steady. We've got this."

2. Mental Audits

Pause and ask:

- What am I holding that's not mine?

- What's loud in my head that doesn't deserve the volume?

- What decision am I avoiding?

Name it. Write it. Or just say it out loud in the car, in your office, wherever you can catch a breath.

Mental audits aren't about fixing — they're about noticing. Clarity starts with awareness.

3. Micro-Journaling

Don't overcomplicate it. Just grab a notepad or open your Notes app and answer this: "What do I need to get out of my head right now?"

Let it spill. It can be messy. It doesn't have to be pretty. The point is to move the mental clutter out of your brain and into a container that's not you.

Creating a 10-Minute Buffer Zone

You need decompression time — not just after work, but in between moments that demand different versions of you.

Going from a layoff meeting to a one-on-one check-in? That's not a seamless shift — that's emotional whiplash.

Create a **10-minute buffer zone**. Block it on your calendar. Use it to:

- Breathe

- Stretch

- Walk a loop around the building

- Journal two sentences

- Sit in silence and do nothing

This isn't a luxury. It's maintenance.

You can't show up well when your brain is backlogged.

These small reset windows preserve your clarity — which protects everything else.

Reclaiming Headspace

Clarity isn't just about tools — it's about permission. You have to stop treating your head like a storage unit for everyone else's junk.

Here's how to reclaim it:

- Say **"Let me get back to you" more**. You don't owe instant decisions.

- **Mute notifications during focused work**. Interruptions destroy clarity.

- **Write things down instead of holding them.** Memory is not a filing cabinet.

- **Turn off helpful-mode after hours**. You're not on-call for the world.

Mental clarity is often lost in small, invisible leaks. Boundaries patch those leaks. Rest restores the flow. And tools like breathwork and journaling keep your mind from getting jammed.

This chapter isn't asking you to do more — it's giving you permission to do less noise, less chaos, less overdrive.

Because you think better when you breathe.

You lead better when you pause.

And you live better when your mind isn't constantly buffering.

Chapter 8

Reconnecting with Your 'Why'

If you've ever asked yourself, "How did I even end up here?" — you're not alone.

HR has a way of pulling you into the weeds. Policies. Paperwork. Pings. Problems. Another meeting. Another tough conversation. Another new fire to manage before you've even had your coffee.

And somewhere in the middle of all that... your why gets buried.

This chapter is about digging it back up.

More Than a Job Description

You didn't get into HR to manage PTO policies and track compliance checklists. That might be part of the role — but it's not the heart of it.

Somewhere early on, something lit you up:

- Maybe it was watching people grow into leadership.

- Maybe it was helping someone find their footing after a hard season.

- Maybe it was believing that workplaces could actually be better — and wanting to be part of that change.

Whatever it was, it probably wasn't just about rules and reports. It was about *people*.

The problem is, over time, purpose gets buried under process. And before long, you're surviving the day instead of shaping the experience.

But here's the thing: **your why didn't leave you. It's just quiet right now.**

What Made You Choose This?

Let's go back for a second.

What drew you to this work? Was it:

- A personal experience you wanted to do differently?

- A desire to be the advocate you didn't have?

- A deep belief that people deserve to feel seen, safe, and supported at work?

Those answers matter. They're not cheesy. They're the root system that holds you steady when everything above the surface is chaotic.

Take five minutes and ask yourself:

- "What part of HR do I love — even when it's hard?"

- "When do I feel most aligned with my purpose?"

- "If I had to describe why I do this work in one sentence, what would it be?"

Write it down. Say it out loud. Let it ground you.

Aligning Your Role With Your Values (Again)

You can't always control your org's culture, your leadership's behavior, or the structure you work inside. But you can bring your values to the front — and use them to shape how you show up.

If you value fairness, how are you showing that in the gray areas?

If you value dignity, how are you advocating for it during offboarding or discipline?

If you value growth, are you modeling it in how you develop yourself — not just others?

You don't need a title change to realign. You need *intention*. You need to lead from your why — even in the smallest decisions.

That's where meaning returns.

When the Why Shifts

Sometimes, your original why no longer fits. That doesn't mean you're lost — it means you've evolved.

You might realize:

- You care more about coaching than compliance now.

- You want to shift into DEI work, or org development, or strategy.

- You're not the same person you were when you started this path — and that's okay.

Reconnecting with your why doesn't always mean going backward. It can mean giving yourself permission to dream forward.

To say: *This version of me needs something different — and that's not failure. That's growth.*

Your why is your compass. Not your job title. Not your company's mission statement. Not your resume.

Your *why* is what brings you back to center when everything else feels off.

So pause. Listen for it. Rewrite it if you need to.

And remember: you don't have to *find* purpose. You just have to stop ignoring it.

Chapter 9

Micro-Rituals for Resilience

You don't need a two-week vacation to reset your nervous system. You need about two minutes — done consistently.

Resilience isn't about being bulletproof. It's about recovery. It's about being able to move through chaos without being consumed by it. And in HR, where stress is always in reach, you can't wait for peace to find you. You have to *build* it into your day — on purpose.

That's where micro-rituals come in.

What Is a Micro-Ritual?

A micro-ritual is a small, intentional action that tells your nervous system: *We're safe. We're steady. We're in control.*

It's not self-care in the performative, social-media way. It's not a spa day or a scented candle. It's a *signal* — one that breaks the stress cycle and resets your internal rhythm.

These rituals are fast. Repeatable. Sustainable. And when practiced consistently, they become your armor.

Stabilizing Your Nervous System

Here's what stress does:
- It locks your jaw.

- It shortens your breath.

- It makes your shoulders creep up toward your ears.

- It hijacks your ability to think clearly.

But here's the good news: *the body can't stay in high alert when it's grounded.* You just have to show it how to come back down.

Try these:

1. The Ground Check (1 Minute)

- Plant your feet flat on the floor.

- Press your toes and heels down.

- Take a slow breath and say (out loud or in your head): "I'm here. I'm safe. I can handle this."

2. Box Breathing (2 Minutes)

- Inhale for 4 seconds

- Hold for 4 seconds

- Exhale for 4 seconds

- Hold for 4 seconds

- Repeat for 4–5 rounds

3. Body Scan (While Sitting at Your Desk)

Start at the top of your head and slowly scan downward. Relax each part: jaw, shoulders, hands, stomach, thighs, calves. By the time you reach your feet, your body has softened and your mind has slowed.

Grounding Routines That Stick

You don't need 17 steps. You need 1–3 *rituals* that you repeat so often, they become non-negotiable.

Here are some that actually work in the real world:

- **Morning Cue**: Light a candle, stretch for 3 minutes, or open your blinds and drink water before checking your phone. The point is to *start with presence*, not panic.

- **Lunch Reset**: Eat away from your screen. Even for 10 minutes. Let your nervous system *rest* before the next round of reactivity.

- **Commute Decompression**: No emails on the drive home. Instead, use music, silence, or a short podcast to signal the shift from "HR mode" to "human mode."

- **End-of-Day Closure**: Write down 3 things you handled well — even if they were tiny. This rewires your brain to recognize completion, instead of obsessing over what's unfinished.

Repeat these rituals enough and your body starts to anticipate relief — instead of bracing for more.

Protecting Your Energy Proactively

Resilience doesn't start when you're falling apart. It starts before the crisis hits.

Protect your energy like it's part of your job — because it is.
- Say no before you're drained.

- Take breaks before you're burned out.

- Interrupt stress early — not after it explodes.

- Keep rituals simple enough that you can do them even on your worst day.

Think of micro-rituals as *preparation*, not repair. You don't wait to drink water until you're dehydrated — you sip it all day. Same with your sanity.

You won't always feel strong. You won't always feel balanced. But resilience isn't about how calm you look — it's about how quickly you come back to center.

And you don't need a major life overhaul to build that.

You just need a few small rituals. Done consistently. With intention. That's how you protect your peace in a job that pulls at it constantly.

Chapter 10

From Overloaded to Empowered

Let's talk about real power.

Not title power. Not corner office power. Internal power — the kind that holds steady even when you're being challenged, dismissed, or undervalued.

The kind that doesn't need permission to show up fully.

Many HR professionals live in a near-constant state of internal pressure. The need to prove we belong. To be twice as polished. To never mess up.

And here's the truth no one wants to say out loud: **we carry imposter syndrome more than we admit.**

Even with the credentials. Even with years of experience. Even when we're the one others come to for answers — *we still question our own authority.*

The Imposter in the Mirror

You know the voice:

"Who am I to speak up here?"

"What if I get this wrong?"

"Maybe I'm not as good as they think I am."

That voice isn't truth. It's fear. Fear fed by systems that haven't always valued our seat at the table. Fear reinforced by roles that ask us to lead without always giving us full power to make decisions.

The imposter voice is what keeps us overcompensating. It drives perfectionism, people-pleasing, and burnout. It convinces us that rest is laziness, that boundaries are risky, that one misstep will ruin our credibility.

But that voice doesn't get to run your career anymore.

What Empowerment Actually Looks Like

Empowerment isn't about being loud. It's about being anchored.

It's knowing your worth without needing to hustle for it. It's making decisions without apologizing for your presence. It's understanding that you belong — even when you feel doubt.

You can be confident and still nervous. You can be seasoned and still growing. You can be powerful without pretending you're perfect.

True empowerment means:

- Saying "I don't know" without shame

- Holding a boundary without explanation

- Letting go of the need to constantly prove yourself

It's being grounded enough to take feedback, advocate for yourself, and trust your own voice.

Let This Be Your Shift

Start interrupting the imposter narrative. When that voice pipes up, respond with facts:

- "I have helped people through hard things. I know what I'm doing."

- "It's okay to learn as I lead."

- "I've earned my place — and I don't need to over-explain why."

You are not here by accident. You didn't stumble into this career. You've built it — through empathy, resilience, and showing up day after day. Let this be the chapter where you release the pressure to be flawless. And reclaim the power of being fully, unapologetically capable.

Because *you are*.

Chapter 11
Culture Starts with You

Let's get something clear: culture isn't a mission statement. It's not a company slogan or a slide deck shared at orientation.

Culture is what people feel safe to say. It's how people treat each other under pressure. It's how much space people have to be human — including you.

And here's the truth most people miss: culture doesn't start with policies. **It starts with presence**.

That means it starts with you.

The Way You Show Up Matters

You don't have to be the CHRO to influence culture. You don't need an org-wide title to model what healthy looks like. In fact, the most powerful change agents are often the quiet ones — the people others observe and think:

- "They actually take lunch and don't apologize for it."

- "They held a boundary and didn't get flustered."

- "They shut down gossip without shame or drama."

That's culture work.

When you create calm, when you model respect, when you treat people with dignity — especially when it's hard — you're shaping the environment around you, without saying a word.

Culture Is Contagious

We know negativity spreads fast in workplaces. But here's the flip side: **so does clarity. So does calm. So does courage.**

You start showing up more grounded, more centered, more unapologetic about your limits — and others take notice. Not everyone, but the right ones will.

One person modeling healthier behavior gives others permission to do the same.

This isn't about being perfect. It's about being real. It's about showing what it looks like to lead with emotional intelligence without emotional exhaustion.

What You Can Normalize

As an HR professional (or anyone in a support role) , you have an opportunity to normalize what's often treated as "optional" but is actually essential:

- Pausing before responding

- Naming burnout without shame

- Asking for time to process hard news

- Setting limits on emotional labor

- Declining things that don't align with your capacity

Every time you do this, you're teaching the people around you what's possible.

Culture Doesn't Shift by Itself

And yes — sometimes it feels like no one's watching. Like your efforts don't matter. But culture doesn't shift with a bang. It moves like water. Quiet. Persistent. Unshakable over time.

You might be the first one to act differently. That's okay. Someone has to go first.

Let it be you.

Let how you carry yourself be the change you wish existed.

Because every workplace change — every new norm, every healthier way of being — starts with one person deciding:

"I won't play by burnout rules anymore."

Chapter 12

Designing a Sustainable Career in HR

Let's say it clearly: You can stay in this field and not burn out.

You *can* have a meaningful, respected, values-aligned career in HR — *without* being the emotional dumping ground, the 24/7 fixer, or the quiet martyr for company culture.

But it has to be by design. Not default.

Sustainability Means Systems

A sustainable HR career isn't about avoiding stress completely. It's about building the systems — internally and externally — that protect your peace and energy over the long haul.

This means:

- Defining what "enough" looks like for *you* — not for your boss, or your team, or your LinkedIn feed

- Creating career goals that include *well-being* as a success metric

- Normalizing recovery, sabbaticals, and strategic rest

If your career path doesn't include space for healing and re-centering, it's not a path — it's a trap.

Future-Proofing Your Role

Ask yourself:
- What kind of work do I want to be doing in 5 years?

- What boundaries need to be in place for that to feel *sustainable*?

- What support or development do I need to grow without overextending?

Then ask: Who in your circle helps you hold that vision? If the answer is "no one," it's time to build that support system. Coaches, mentors, therapists, peer HR professionals — you need people who see you, not just your output.

Staying Doesn't Mean Settling

You don't have to leave HR to save yourself. You also don't have to stay in toxic, unrewarding, or misaligned environments out of fear.
Sustainability means:
- Knowing when to pivot

- Trusting your gut about culture fit

- Believing that *you are the asset*, not the position

You've earned the right to build your career around your values. That includes being ambitious *and* peaceful.

Design with Intention

A sustainable career in HR is one where you:
- Have clear personal and professional boundaries

- Work in alignment with your values

- Continue learning without running yourself into the ground

- Leave work at work more often than not

- See yourself as a person first, professional second

This chapter isn't just an ending — it's a design prompt. Build a version of your career that makes space for *you* to thrive.

Because you deserve to grow, not just survive.

Let's close it out.

Conclusion: Your Exit Interview with Stress

If you've made it this far, then let's take a breath — a real one. In through the nose. Out through the mouth. Let the shoulders drop.

This is the moment you get to say: *enough.*

Not because you're giving up. Not because you can't handle it. But because you're choosing something better. More honest. More human. More sustainable.

This book has not been about quitting HR. It's been about quitting the pressure to be everything for everyone. Quitting the idea that your value is in how much you absorb. Quitting the myth that your professionalism depends on your self-neglect.

You're not just allowed to unplug — **you're expected to**. You're not just allowed to set boundaries — **you're required to**. You're not just allowed to take care of yourself — **you're *responsible* for it**.

And when you do, you model something powerful for everyone watching: That it's possible to care without carrying everything. That it's possible to lead without losing yourself. That it's possible to be strong and still need space.

This is your exit interview with stress. Not with the profession. Not with your purpose. Just with the version of the role that demands more than you were ever meant to give.

Walk forward lighter. Clearer. Freer. You've done enough. You are enough. And your peace is not up for negotiation.

Let that be the new norm. Let you be the new standard.

Close the book. Take a deep breath. And end the exit interview by wishing stress all the best in its future endeavors.

Appendix

30-Day "Unburden" Challenge

Small, practical prompts to help you reset your stress habits and build emotional resilience — one day at a time.

WEEK 1: Awareness

Day 1: Name your biggest stress source at work.

Day 2: Pay attention to your posture during stress.

Day 3: Track every interruption today — and how it made you feel.

Day 4: Write one thing you're proud of this week.

Day 5: Identify a boundary you've been avoiding.

Day 6: Breathe intentionally for 2 minutes between meetings.

Day 7: Say no (or "not right now") at least once.

WEEK 2: Boundaries in Action

Day 8: Tell someone what your working hours really are.

Day 9: Block time for lunch — and take it.

Day 10: Rewrite one "I have to" into "I choose to."

Day 11: Practice saying "I'm at capacity" out loud.

Day 12: Let a non-urgent task wait.

Day 13: Shut down your computer at a set time.

Day 14: Notice how your body feels when you protect your time.

WEEK 3: Reconnection

Day 15: Revisit your original "why" for doing this work.

Day 16: Celebrate something small you did well today.

Day 17: Have a conversation that's honest, not just polite.

Day 18: Reconnect with someone who supports you.

Day 19: Reflect on a moment where you felt like you made a difference.

Day 20: Write down 3 qualities you bring to your team.

Day 21: Do one thing today just for *you*.

WEEK 4: Moving Differently

Day 22: Delegate something — even if you think you could "just do it faster."

Day 23: Leave on time. Period.

Day 24: Build in a 3-minute buffer between commitments.

Day 25: Protect your peace in one conversation today.

Day 26: Try a micro-ritual from Chapter 9.

Day 27: Give yourself permission to *not fix it*.

Day 28: Look at your calendar — remove one thing that doesn't serve you.

Day 29: End your day with one deep breath and a full stop.

Day 30: Reflect: What are you no longer available for?

Burnout Warning Signs Checklist

Use this checklist as an early detection tool. Burnout rarely announces itself with a bang — it creeps in silently, disguising itself as fatigue, detachment, or "just a rough week."

Check off any that apply:

Physical & Mental Fatigue *

Emotional Drain *

Relationship Withdrawal *

Disengagement & Cynicism *

Behavioral Shifts *

What to do if you check off several?

1. **Pause** — not to judge yourself, but to   acknowledge reality.

2. **Name it** — "This might be burnout" is a   powerful sentence.

3. **Act** — Pick one thing to change this   week (refer back to Chapter 9 or the 30-Day Challenge).

Burnout isn't weakness. It's an alarm. And the good news is: you're listening.

Sample Scripts for Hard Conversations

Sometimes the hardest part of boundary-setting or change-making is finding the right words. Here are real-world examples you can adapt to your style and situation.

Setting a Boundary with a Manager

"I want to continue supporting the team effectively, and that means being intentional with my energy. Right now, I'm at capacity. Can we look at prioritization together?"

"In order to deliver well on my current responsibilities, I need to pass on this additional ask. Can we revisit it next quarter or look at who else might be available?"

Redirecting Emotional Dumping

"I want to make sure you get the support you need, and this sounds like something our EAP or a counselor could really help with. Let me connect you."

"I hear how much this is weighing on you. I want to make sure I stay in my lane and point you toward the best resources for this."

Naming Burnout (Without Apologizing for It)

"I've been noticing signs of burnout in myself and I want to be proactive about it — not just for me, but so I can keep showing up at my best."

"I need to step back and reset. I'm prioritizing sustainability in how I work, and that means recalibrating some things."

Saying No Without Guilt

"I appreciate you thinking of me — I'm going to have to decline so I can protect my focus on what's already on my plate."

"That's not something I can take on right now. Let's talk through other options."

Having a Career Check-In

"I want to check in on where I'm headed and how aligned I am with what matters to me in this role. Can we schedule time to talk big picture?"

"I've been reflecting on where I add the most value and what keeps me engaged. I'd love to share some thoughts and hear your perspective."

Scripts aren't meant to be read word-for-word. They're training wheels. Use them to practice new language, try on new boundaries, and hold your ground with more clarity and confidence.

Self-Reflection Prompts & Tools

These prompts are designed to help you pause, notice, and gently reconnect to what matters — especially when you feel lost in the noise.

Use them in a journal, voice memo, or during a quiet walk. No pressure. No grading. Just truth.

Personal Check-Ins

What am I holding today that isn't mine?

Where in my day do I most lose track of myself?

What have I been needing — and not saying?

When was the last time I felt proud of how I handled something?

Stress Inventory

What patterns of stress do I notice lately? (Timing, people, tasks, themes)

Am I responding to everything like it's an emergency?

What boundary is asking to be set or reinforced?

What am I afraid will happen if I stop overfunctioning?

Career Alignment

Does this version of my career still fit me?

Where am I compromising too much?

What values are non-negotiable for me now?

How do I define "success" — and has that changed?

◻ Tools for Clarity

Daily Debrief: What went well? What drained me? What did I learn?

"Stress Dump" Page: Write everything that's bothering you — then sort it into: Mine / Not Mine / Let It Go.

Visualize: What does *lightness* look like at work? What do you look like unburdened?

About the author

**Jason Michaels, MBA, SPHR, SHRM-CP**, is an HR leader, consultant, and author with more than twelve years of hands-on experience in human resources leadership. He currently serves as the Human Resources Manager for the Bedford Regional Water Authority in Virginia, where he focuses on people-first practices, organizational culture, and leadership development.

Jason holds a Bachelor of Science in Psychology from Fayetteville State University and a Master of Business Administration with concentrations in Human Resources, Project Management, and Entrepreneurial Leadership. He is credentialed as a Senior Professional in Human Resources (SPHR) and as a Certified Professional by the Society for Human Resource Management (SHRM-CP).

Jason is passionate about helping HR professionals and leaders move beyond survival mode. His work centers on making the invisible emotional load of HR visible, manageable, and less isolating. Through practical tools and compassionate insight, he equips others to thrive in the field they love—without losing themselves in the process.